Contents

Introduction

Over the last century, the way we feed ourselves has been totally transformed. This change has been driven by the commercialisation of food.

The food we eat has moved from being locally produced, made on a small scale (or home cooked) and sold at local markets and shops to being mass manufactured, globally sourced and sold in supermarkets.

There is convincing evidence that the diet of our ancestors was considerably better than our diet today. In essence, we have become very good at "feeding" ourselves cheaply and conveniently. But in doing so, we often fail to nourish ourselves. This is a basic life skill.

Increasingly, this is being recognised. The obesity epidemic seen in the USA (and becoming a problem in the rest of the developed world) is well documented. There are a number of people starting to speak out about these issues and the many related topics.

In response, **COOK** has been researching this area - as a food producer and retailer, we believe we have a responsibility to take it extremely seriously.

In essence, we have become very good at "feeding" ourselves cheaply and conveniently. But in doing so, we often fail to nourish ourselves. This is a basic life skill.

What this guide is about...

We have taken an objective look at the area of health and nutrition by researching all of the different (and often polemic) points of view out there. We have spoken to various experts: nutritionists, scientists, farmers, fishmongers, greengrocers and so on. We have read everything we can, and looked at loads of websites.

"Doubting everything and believing everything are two equally convenient solutions that guard us from having to think."

- Henri Poincare

In the **COOK** spirit of saving you time without compromising on quality (!), we have tried to distil the most important - and often misunderstood - bits of information and give you some pointers about where to go if you're keen to find out more.

If you want to learn more about the nutritional content of **COOK** food, turn to Part V where we talk about the many health benefits of how **COOK** does things!

COOK has always been about food that looks and tastes as though you made it at home. There is no sense in which we want to take the pleasure out of food and drink. Hell would have to freeze over. Enjoyment of good food & wine, and good health through good diet can coexist. The French have been doing it for years! But it does require balance.

As always with these things, "the devil is in the detail". Welcome to our Nutrition Guide. We hope that you enjoy it and are able to use it to help ensure you have a healthy diet.

Part I – The Problem:
Overfed and Undernourished

Food is more than a matter of taste - it is fuel for the body. And more than fuel: it provides the body with the basic nutrients needed for good health. All too often, the food we eat is made up of "empty calories": food that keeps us going but is otherwise stripped of the vital nutrients that nourish our bodies and keep them healthy.

If we are going to learn how to nourish ourselves, we need to develop a basic understanding of what our nutritional needs are, and the impact food has on our health.

> Food is more than fuel for the body:
>
> It provides us with the basic nutrients for healthy living.

Where we have gone wrong...

- We eat too much of the wrong types of carbohydrates (**"fast releasing carbohydrates"**) including too much sugar, and too little of the right type of carbohydrates (**"slow releasing carbohydrates"**).

- Our diet is too high in unhealthy fats: we consume too many **saturated fats**, **trans fats** and **hydrogenated fats**. Our diet is too low in healthy **monounsaturated fats** and essential **polyunsaturated fats**.

- We eat too much in the way of protein that is also high in saturated fat (e.g. red meat) and too little of the high quality lean sources of protein (e.g. fish and chicken).

- We eat too little nutrient-rich fruit, vegetables and salad.

- We ingest too many **"anti-nutrients"**.

- We still don't drink enough water.

Don't worry if you're not sure what any of the highlighted terms mean - we'll explain them all in a bit...

Tip: Exercise

Food is only one component of healthy living - and exercise is more than merely a way to control or lose weight. It improves chances of longevity by protecting against cardiovascular disease, lowers blood pressure, cholesterol levels, the risk of cancer, osteoporosis, arthritis... the list is endless!

Changing Diets over Time

10,000 years ago, as hunter gathers, our diets were rich in whole grains, nuts, seeds, fibrous roots, fruits and berries. This diet provided a highly nutritious, balanced and sustained energy source.

Today's modern diet, on the other hand, is heavily weighted towards highly-refined foods, sugary foods, high fat processed foods, and red meat.

Take a look at how things have deteriorated...

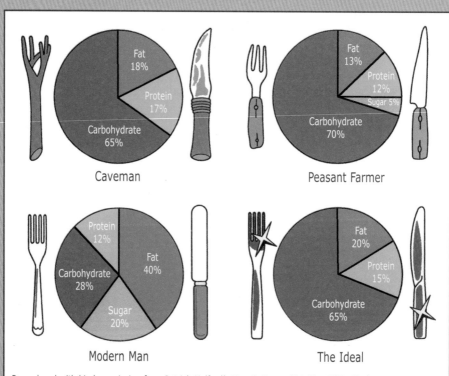

Caveman
- Fat 18%
- Protein 17%
- Carbohydrate 65%

Peasant Farmer
- Fat 13%
- Protein 12%
- Sugar 5%
- Carbohydrate 70%

Modern Man
- Protein 12%
- Fat 40%
- Carbohydrate 28%
- Sugar 20%

The Ideal
- Fat 20%
- Protein 15%
- Carbohydrate 65%

Reproduced with kind permission from Patrick Holford's New Optimum Nutrition Bible. Piatkus

Part II
How to Nourish Ourselves

Good nutrition is the foundation of good health. Food provides us with six basic nutrients:

- Water
- Carbohydrates
- Proteins
- Fats
- Vitamins
- Minerals

Each of these are essential to life.

Water

The human body is two-thirds water. Water is an essential nutrient that is involved in every body process.
It helps to:

- Transport nutrients around the body
- Eliminate toxins
- Aid digestion & absorption
- Utilise water-soluble vitamins
- Maintain body temperature.

We need to aim for 8x250ml glasses of water a day (preferably bottled or filtered) in order to maintain good health.

Carbohydrates

What's their job?

Carbohydrates are the body's main source of fuel. The body can only extract what it needs from carbohydrates (energy) when they have been converted by the body into glucose. Some carbohydrates are converted more rapidly than others.

It is the refined carbohydrates, sugary foods or "fast releasing carbohydrates" that break down rapidly and are absorbed very quickly into the bloodstream. Complex carbohydrates, or "slow releasing carbohydrates", on the other hand, are broken down much more slowly.

Fast releasing carbohydrates

e.g. white pasta, white bread, sugar, sugary foods, white flour, cakes, biscuits, refined flour and fruit juices

Slow releasing carbohydrates

e.g. whole grains, vegetables and fruits

Where have we gone wrong and why does it matter?

We eat too many "fast releasing carbohydrates" and too few "slow releasing carbohydrates". The result is that our body's blood sugar level gets totally out of kilter. To use an analogy, by consuming so many "fast releasing carbohydrates" we put our bodies on the energy equivalent of a rollercoaster ride with highs and lows that leave it utterly exhausted. What our body needs is a constant supply of "slow releasing sugars" that provide the energy equivalent of "cruise control": a constant supply of fuel to keep us ticking over. **If you only learn one thing from this guide, learn that balancing blood sugar is fundamental to good health.**

"The control of blood sugar is one of the most fundamental requirements for a healthy life"

- Sarah Tanksley

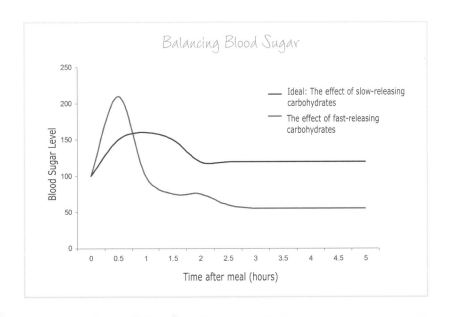

Balancing Blood Sugar

Ideal: The effect of slow-releasing carbohydrates

The effect of fast-releasing carbohydrates

Blood Sugar Level

Time after meal (hours)

Type II Diabetes

An emerging diet-related health problem is Type II Diabetes, also known as "adult onset diabetes" - caused when the body loses its ability to balance sugar levels. The onset of this condition can be the result of a diet high in sugary foods and fast releasing carbohydrates. Type II Diabetes or "adult-onset" diabetes is now being found, for the first time, in children. This is a barometer of the extent to which our modern diet has deteriorated. Type II Diabetes has also been associated with Coronary Heart Disease and neurological disease.

Addicted to Sugar?

There is growing evidence that sugar is addictive: the more sugary or "fast releasing" carbohydrates we eat, the more we crave. No wonder we find it difficult to switch the emphasis in our diet towards slow releasing carbohydrates!

The Glycaemic Index

The Glycaemic Index (G.I.) is a useful concept as it measures how rapidly a carbohydrate is absorbed and its effect on blood sugar elevations. All foods are on a continuum between fast releasing at one end and slow releasing at the other. The G.I. marks where the food is on that continuum.

Foods with a lower G.I. are better. This is because they release their sugars more slowly, meaning that they are generally more filling, more sustaining and they help more with hunger control and appetite. Ultimately, they help to balance blood sugar levels.

Not only will we hear more and more about the G.I., but we will also start hearing a lot about the Glycaemic Load (or G.L.). The G.L. is in many ways a more relevant measure as it takes into account both the type and volume of carbohydrate consumed. For example, a watermelon has a high G.I., but an average portion size provides a low G.L. You should aim to increase your intake of both low G.I. and low G.L. foods.

Tip! Eating some protein with a fast releasing carbohydrate can slow down the speed of the sugar release into the bloodstream. e.g. Some grilled chicken with white pasta will help to balance the effect of the faster releasing sugar release from the white pasta.

Did you know? Tea, coffee, alcohol and stress can all provoke blood sugar fluctuations via adrenaline as the 'fight/flight' mechanism is activated.

Strategy for balancing blood sugar levels:

- Breakfast is the most important meal for balancing blood sugar levels throughout the day

- Eat regular meals containing complex carbohydrates (wholegrains, vegetables and salad)

- Include some protein with each meal

- Avoid (or eat in moderation) high-glycaemic foods (refined foods, sugary foods, processed foods, white bread, starches)

- Limit alcohol and stimulants such as tea and coffee

- Manage stress!

If you learn one thing from this guide, learn that balancing blood sugar is fundamental to good health!

If you want to understand more about the G.I., please read "The G.I. Guide" - Rick Gallop and Hamish Renton

Protein

What's its job?

The word protein is derived from the Greek word 'protos' meaning first. Protein is the basic material of all living cells, and as such is often referred to as "the building block of life". Protein is made up of a group of amino acids, eight of which are "essential" - and therefore extremely important because the body is unable to manufacture them itself. Protein's primary use by the body is for the growth and repair of cells.

Complete Protein

Animal forms of protein (meat, fish, eggs, milk, cheese) contain all eight essential amino acids and are therefore known as "complete" proteins.

Incomplete Protein

Plant proteins (such as tofu - from soya, beans and pulses) generally do not contain all eight essential amino acids and are therefore known as "incomplete" proteins. However, a complete protein can be made from vegetable sources by combining a wholegrain and a plant protein.

Where have we gone wrong and why does it matter?

- Although it is important to eat a full range of complete proteins, it must be remembered that some sources of protein are high in saturated fat - red meat and dairy products in particular (see page 19 on Saturated Fats).

- As a result of some modern farming practices the protein that we consume can contain too many antibiotic and pesticide residues. These are anti-nutrients and are damaging to good health (see page 39 on Anti-nutrients).

- High protein diets can be acid-forming - especially diets high in red meat. This can result in calcium being taken from the bones to 'buffer' the effects of the increased acidity, leading to higher risk of osteoporosis.

Strategy for Protein:

- Emphasise lean sources of protein: fish, chicken, turkey, beans and lentils

- Be discerning about the provenance of the meat and dairy produce you eat

- Eat red meat in moderation - 2 or 3 times a week is a good rule of thumb.

Fats

What's their job?

- Help the body to absorb fat soluble vitamins A,D,E and K.
- Major source of fuel for the body.
- Provide protection around vital organs (e.g. heart and kidney).
- Essential for normal brain development in children and good mental health for us all ... (the brain is 40% fat).

"Fat is good for you! Eating the right amount of the right type of fat is absolutely essential for your wellbeing."

- Patrick Holford, The New Optimium Nutrition Bible

Where have we gone wrong and why does it matter?

Fat is often demonised as a totally bad thing. The truth is that fat is an essential nutrient for the body. The problem is that we are currently consuming far too many saturated fats and not nearly enough polyunsaturated and monounsaturated fats. We are also consuming damaging trans fats and hydrogenated fats - fats which never existed in nature but are a product of some mass manufacturing processes. We need to eliminate these from our diet wherever possible.

Fat Strategy:

- Decrease foods that are high in saturated fat
- Avoid foods containing trans or hydrogenated fats
- Use Olive Oil or Grape Seed Oil in cooking
- Use other polyunsaturated fats such as sunflower, walnut, and sesame oils in salad dressings
- Increase intake of oily fish (mackerel, sardines, salmon): try to eat them at least twice a week to boost your intake of healthy Omega 3 and Omega 6 essential fatty acids.

Saturated Fats

These are the kind found in abundance in fats and oils that are often solid at room temperatures such as:

- Cheese
- Butter
- Animal fat

They are also found in abundance in cream and other dairy products.

 The body actually needs a little saturated fat. However, because so many foods we eat today are high in saturated fat, we really don't need to worry about "adding it to our plate"

Saturated Fats:

 Can block the body's uptake and use of essential fats

 Are used by the body to manufacture cholesterol

 Are strongly associated with Coronary Heart Disease when consumed in excess

Are high in calories - and our sedentary lifestyle means that we do not metabolise saturated fats as well as our ancestors might have done.

Did you know?
Most foods that contain fat, generally have a balance of all three types of fat (saturated, polyunsaturated and monounsaturated). Some are just higher in one type than others.

Monounsaturated Fats

Found in abundance in olives, almonds and their oils, peanuts, hazelnuts, avocado.

 May lessen the risk of heart disease.

 Help to lower cholesterol levels in the blood.

 Believed to offer protection against certain cancers, such as breast and colon cancer.

 Typically high in Vitamin E, the antioxidant vitamin in short supply in many Western diets.

 High in calories.

Polyunsaturated Fats

Found in abundance in fish, nuts, seeds and their oils - for example sunflower oil, walnut oil, sesame oil etc.

 Contain Essential Fatty Acids Omega 3 and Omega 6 (see page 22).

 Boost metabolism and help with nutrient transport.

 Help to lower cholesterol levels in the blood.

 Boost immunity.

 High in calories.

 Unfortunately, polyunsaturated fats are chemically extremely delicate and their healthy benefit can easily be lost through exposure to extremes in heat or light. See Oil and Smoke Points on page 23 for more.

Trans/Hydrogenated Fats

- Found in most processed foods, fast-food, bought cakes, biscuits, crackers, cake and pancake mixes, chips, crisps, fried foods.

- Formed when unsaturated oils are altered through hydrogenation - a process to harden liquid vegetable oils into solids (e.g. during the process of making margarine).

- Not listed on labels - a good thing to remember is that if the ingredient list includes anything "hydrogenated" it's best left on shelf!

- No nutritional benefits.

- The body is not able to use fat in this form.

- The process of hydrogenation changes the chemical structure of essential fatty acids, Omega 3 and Omega 6.

- Toxins or "anti-nutrients" may be present in hydrogenated fats as a result of the hydrogenation process.

- Increase the risk of heart disease and other degenerative diseases.

- Trans fats increase cholesterol levels in the body and decrease beneficial high density lipoprotein (HDL) - increasing the risk of coronary heart disease (see page 25).

- Trans fats interfere with the liver's detoxification system.

- Trans fats inhibit the body's uptake of essential fatty acids, Omega 3 and Omega 6.

What's all this about Omega 3 and Omega 6? (aka Essential Fatty Acids)

Polyunsaturated fats are made up of 2 types of "essential fatty acids" called Omega 3 and Omega 6. They are "essential" because the body cannot produce them itself, therefore they must come from our diet. Every cell in the body needs essential fatty acids for rebuilding and maintaining cell structure. Most of us are far more deficient in Omega 3 than Omega 6 - possibly to a ratio of 4:1.

Main sources of Omega 3

Oily fish (sardines, salmon, mackerel), flaxseed (linseed), walnuts, eggs.

Main sources of Omega 6

Nuts and seeds, and their oils

Essential "Thinny" Acids...?

People usually worry about increasing the amount of fat in their diet for fear of putting on weight. However, it has been found that eating more of the healthy essential fatty acids, Omega 3 and Omega 6, actually helps people lose weight by boosting metabolism, helping you to burn calories more efficiently and improving nutrient transport. Dr Gillian McKeith (presenter of the TV Series "You Are What You Eat", and author of the book of the same name) likes to call Essential Fatty Acids, Essential "Thinny" Acids so people get the concept!

Did you know?
Oil and Smoke Points

All oils have a different "smoke point": the temperature at which that oil starts to burn and its chemical structure is altered. When this happens, harmful "trans fats" can be formed. Polyunsaturated oils are particularly vulnerable to this because of their volatile chemical structure. The best oils to use during cooking are olive oil and grape seed oil (cooking with butter is also fine but watch out for high levels of saturated fat). All other nut and seed oils are excellent sources of Essential Fatty Acids - but it's best to use them cold, as salad or vegetable dressings.

Margarine vs Butter?

Although butter is high in saturated fat - and so should not be consumed in excess - it is free of hydrogenated or trans fats that may be present in margarine. Remember, even though the core ingredient of margarine is usually a polyunsaturated oil, such as sunflower oil, the healthy benefit is often lost during the hydrogenation process when the oil is heated to extremely high temperatures.

Did you know?
Sugar is known as the 'fifth fat' because it is turned into fat if the body has not used it for energy. Look out for hidden 'fat' in the form of sugar - especially in so-called 'low-fat' or '0% fat' foods!

What about Cholesterol?

Cholesterol is not a type of fat! Cholesterol is a fat-like substance present in high levels in the skin of some types of meat and egg yolk and other food substances. Cholesterol is needed by the body in small amounts to maintain health: it forms an integral part of cell membranes, helping to hold them together. It also helps make Vitamin D and hormones and is a component of the brain and nervous system.

So what's the problem with Cholesterol?

High levels of cholesterol are strongly associated with cardiovascular disease. Cholesterol cannot be dissolved in the blood and the only mode of transport for cholesterol round the body is by lipoproteins. There are two sorts of lipoproteins: high density lipoproteins (HDL) and low density lipoproteins (LDL). HDL is beneficial as it moves cholesterol to the liver where it can be excreted. LDL on the other hand, transports cholesterol away from the liver, around the body, where it can deposit cholesterol in arteries, contributing to higher risk of heart attacks and strokes.

HDLs are the goodies that can help decrease cholesterol levels.

LDLs are the baddies that increase cholesterol levels.

If you would like to know what your cholesterol levels are, book in at your local Boots who offer free cholesterol checks. Don't forget to look at the ratios of HDL to LDL - this is important in assessing whether or not your health is at risk.

Low in fat, high in fibre and packed full of vitamins and minerals, fruit and vegetables are the key to optimum health.

Vitamins & Minerals

Vitamins and minerals are known as micronutrients yet perhaps they should be thought of as "little powerhouses" - it is difficult to overestimate their importance for good health. A diet rich in vitamins and minerals, compared to a diet poor in these vital nutrients, is a bit like the difference between growing your plants in rich compost rather than ordinary soil.

Vitamins – What's their job?

- Regulate metabolism.
- Assist in the biochemical processes that allow the body to take what it needs from food.
- Assist enzymes, the essential chemicals at the root of all bodily functions. Vitamins work in synergy, making sure that all body activities are carried out as they should be.

Fat Soluble Vitamins

Can be stored by the body in fat tissue and the liver.

e.g. Vitamins A, D, E, K

Insoluble Vitamins

Cannot be stored by the body so should be eaten daily.

e.g. B Vitamins, Vitamin C

Minerals – What's their job?

- Ensure the proper composition of body fluids.
- Allow the formation of blood and bones.
- Are important for a healthy nervous system.
- Are vital for muscle health, including the cardiovascular system (the heart and its workings).
- Like vitamins: assist enzymes in all body functions.

Some examples of minerals: Calcium, Magnesium, Potassium, Phosphorus, Boron, Chromium, Copper, Zinc, Iodine, Iron, Manganese, Selenium, Calcium.

Where have we gone wrong?

As we've said before, the emphasis in our diet on highly processed food results in a diet stripped of the vital vitamins and minerals that occur naturally in the component materials of our food.

Vitamins work in synergy, making sure that all body activities are carried out as they should be.

Strategy for boosting the vitamin and mineral content of our diets

- Aim for four portions of vegetables and two portions of fruit a day.

- Eat high quality natural foods instead of factory produced or processed foods.

The Food Doctor: Healing Foods for Mind and Body by Ian Marber and Vicki Edgson, has a good section detailing which vitamins and minerals are found in which foods.

If you want to take vitamin supplements, a good source of vitamin and mineral supplements is BioCare
Tel: 0121 433 3727 or www.biocare.co.uk

Vitamin C is the most vital nutrient for keeping your immune system strong.

Where to get your vitamins and minerals

A well balanced diet containing lots of fruit and vegetables is the best way of ensuring you get a good balance of vitamins and minerals.
Here are some examples:

Vitamin	Good Sources
A	Carrots, broccoli, green leafy vegetables, sweet potatoes
C	Citrus fruit, kiwis, tomatoes, peppers and green vegetables, parsley
B3	Avocado, chicken, tuna, almonds, peanuts
B6	Brown rice, spinach, bananas, avocado, chicken, walnuts
B12	Tuna, shell fish, chicken
D	Vegetable oils, eggs, oily fish
K	Cabbage, kale, spinach, yoghurt

Mineral	Good Sources
Calcium	Green leafy vegetables, spinach, watercress, sesame seeds
Magnesium	Mushrooms, onions, pulses, wholegrains, nuts, green vegetables
Selenium	Avocado, lentils, brazil nuts, salmon
Potassium	Cauliflowers, carrots, cucumbers, parsnips, broccoli, bananas.

Antioxidants and free radicals

Ever heard the phrase "defensive eating"? It's a term used to describe the way that we can improve our body's immunity through our diet. There is a group of vitamins and minerals called "antioxidants" that do just that: defend the body from the harm caused by damaging "free radicals".

What are free radicals and where do they come from?

Free radicals can be extremely dangerous to our health. They may cause damage to cells and this, in turn, accelerates the ageing process, can impair the immune system and increases the risk of infections, cancer, heart disease and other degenerative diseases. Free radicals are formed from any combustion or "oxidation" process including the following:

- Smoking
- Burning of petrol to create exhaust fumes
- Radiation
- Frying or barbecuing food
- Stress.

The process of "oxidation" leads to deterioration, ageing and breakdown of a cell - oxidation is what causes metal to rust, apples to brown, or fats to go rancid.

Our weapon: Antioxidants

The good news is we have a powerful source of protection from free radicals in the form of "antioxidants". Antioxidants disarm the potential damage that a free radical can cause in the body. It's pretty impressive: if an antioxidant is present as a free radical is about to wreak havoc on a cell, the antioxidant brings about bio-chemical processes that literally eject the free radical from the cell, before it causes any damage. The most potent forms of antioxidants are found in the nutrients of brightly coloured fruit and vegetables.

Good sources of antioxidants:

- Citrus Fruit
- Broccoli, cabbage, sprouts
- Red and blue berries
- Red, orange, yellow and dark green fruit and vegetables.

Antioxidants are the "goodies" that neutralise harmful "free radicals". Antioxidants are found in abundance in brightly coloured fruit and vegetables. If your plate is full of colourful vegetables you are probably getting a very good dose of antioxidants!

Needless to say, we should also try to limit our exposure to free radicals wherever possible.

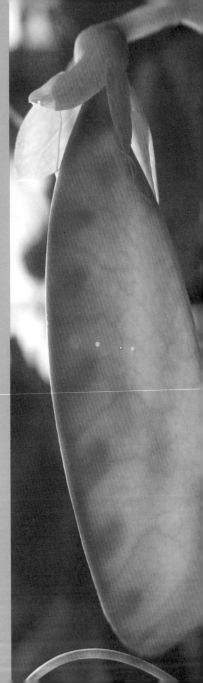

The lifespan of a vegetable

Any fruit or vegetable starts to deteriorate as soon as it is harvested. This is because the plant or tree is literally its lifeline, supplying water and nutrients and keeping it alive. As soon as these essentials are no longer supplied, the fruit or vegetable starts to die. As it does so, valuable minerals and vitamins contained within it start to die also.

It's worth finding out about vegetable boxes from local farms, or visiting local farmers' markets to get fresh produce. This is a good way to make sure the fruit and vegetables you eat are fresh and have not been artificially "kept fresh" by being stored at chilled temperatures for long periods of time.

The greater the age of a fruit or vegetable, the lower its nutritional value

- Buy smaller vegetables rather than those - such as cucumber, cabbage, melons etc - that have been cut in half. As soon as the vegetable or fruit is cut it starts to lose its nutrients.

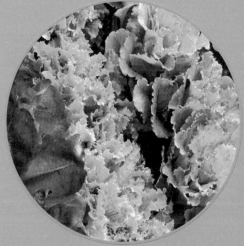

- Avoid pre-prepared vegetables - often they are soaked in chlorine to slow their deterioration.

- Wherever possible, buy little and often.

Tip: Keep broccoli in 'tiptop' condition before use by storing in the fridge with the stalk immersed in a couple of inches of cold water in a glass to keep it hydrated.

For more information on how to treat fruit and vegetables to maximise their nutrient content, try: www.wholefoods.org (health info/nutrition reference library).

Fibre

What's its job?

Fibre is an unequivocally good thing, because it:

- Slows down the absorption of fast releasing carbohydrates by the body, thereby helping to regulate blood sugar levels.
- Lowers cholesterol levels in the blood.
- Binds to toxins and helps eliminate them.
- Helps the body absorb essential vitamins.
- Prevents constipation.
- Influences gut flora - encourages the growth of beneficial bacteria.
- Protects against cancer - in particular bowel cancer by decreasing transit time (no explanation - use your imagination!)
- Lessens likelihood of other diseases of the colon e.g. diverticulitis.

Where have we gone wrong?

Our diets are worryingly deficient in fibre. One manifestation of our failure to have sufficient levels of fibre in our diets is the increasing number of children suffering from constipation. But more broadly, failure to eat sufficient fibre in our diets simply denies us the many benefits it offers us.

Good sources of fibre:

- Fresh fruit and vegetables - eaten raw, they contain even more fibre
- Wholegrains, beans, lentils, chickpeas
- Dried fruits
- Linseed
- Oat bran
- Nuts and seeds.

Did you know?
Fibre encourages the growth of "good bacteria" present in the gut. These are the same "good bacteria" we hear about in live yoghurt.

Did you know?
Fibre & Refined Flour

Fibre naturally occurs in wholegrain (or unrefined) flour. Refined flour, on the other hand, contains little or no fibre. The origins of refined flour came about during the industrial revolution: flour was refined so it would not support weevils, would not go off and, therefore, would provide a cheap fodder for the working masses. However, as with sugar, we have developed a taste for refined flour and our diet is now crammed with foods made with it - depriving us of one major source of fibre.

Salt

Salt is needed by the body for the following vital functions:

- Healthy muscle function
- pH control (acidity vs alkalinity) in the blood
- Blood pressure regulation.

Most people consume more salt than they need, both by adding salt when cooking and adding more salt to food at the table. In addition, many processed foods tend to be high in salt.

Why do we need to cut down on salt?

Eating too much salt can raise your blood pressure. People with high blood pressure or "hypertension" are three times more likely to develop heart disease or have a stroke than people with normal blood pressure. Salt increases blood pressure because it "furs up the arteries" if eaten in excess, making it harder for blood to circulate around the body.

Salt is made up of sodium and chloride. It is the sodium that is bad for your health. This is why many food retailers give the amount of salt in foods as "sodium" on their labels.

Drinking lots of water and eating plenty of fruit and vegetables helps counteract the effects of a diet high in salt. But the best thing to do is to limit the amount of salty foods that you're eating.

www.salt.gov.uk provides an excellent source of information about salt in the diet. Look out for the cartoon that illustrates how salt can "fur up arteries".

Nutrients at a glance

Title	Also known as	Benefits	Examples
Fast releasing carbohydrates	Refined foods and sugars	Few. They are stripped of nutrients or provide "empty calories".	White flour products such as white bread, rice, pasta, cakes, biscuits.
Slow releasing carbohydrates	Complex carbohydrates	Provide dietary fibre - slow sugar absorption. Eliminate toxins. Prevent disease.	Wholegrains (oats, brown rice, wholewheat bread), beans, pulses, fruits, vegetables, salad.
Proteins	Complete Proteins (meat source) Incomplete Proteins (vegetable source)	Help the body build and repair itself. Balance blood sugar levels when eaten with carbohydrates. Vegetable protein contains less saturated fat.	Chicken, fish, lamb, beef, tofu, quinoa, beans, pulses, avocado.
Saturated fat		Small amounts needed by the body.	Red meat and dairy produce.
Polyunsaturated fats	Essential Fats Omega 3 and 6	Needed for all body functions.	Oily fish, flaxseed (linseed), nuts and seeds.
Monounsaturated fats	Omega 9	Helps to lower LDL cholesterol.	Olive and other vegetable and nut oils.
Vitamins and minerals	Micronutrients	Immunity, protection against disease.	Fresh fruits, vegetables and salads, wholegrains, lean meat, fish, eggs, beans, pulses.
Antioxidants	Phytochemicals	Protection against free radical damage.	Red, yellow, orange, green fruits and vegetables. Dark red/blue coloured fruit and vegetables.
Fibre	Roughage	Regulates blood sugar levels. Binds to toxins and helps eliminate them.	Fruit and vegetables, nuts, seeds, wholegrains, beans, pulses.
Salt	Sodium	Fluid balance/muscle health/blood pH/blood pressure regulation.	Added to cooking water or at the table.

Part III – The Body Beseiged
Anti-Nutrients and Toxins

Our diet has become deficient in essential nutrients, as described in Parts I and II.

As a double whammy, the way we live and the way we eat cause us to ingest things that our body has to do battle with. Our systems are therefore put under an extra burden as they try to rid themselves of these harmful substances. And that's before they even start on the job of maintaining good health.

Anti-nutrients and toxins compromise immunity. They are the other side of the coin that explains the recent increasing incidence of food allergies and diet-related health problems.

Anti-nutrients are contaminants that are found in food.

Toxins come from the environment in general.

Sources of Anti-nutrients

Preservatives, Additives, Antibiotics residues, Pesticide and Fertiliser residues, Fried foods, MSG (monosodium glutamate)

Sources of Toxins

Air and Water Pollution, Smoking, Radiation, End Products of the Chemical and Plastics Industry

The effects of these harmful agents are only just coming to light. At best, anti-nutrients add little or no nutritional value to a food product. The body - specifically the liver - has to work incredibly hard to remove them from the body.

At worst, anti-nutrients can pose a threat to health - particularly if consumed in excess - by compromising immunity. It's worth remembering that most artificial ingredients provide benefits to the food vendor - prolonging shelf life or facilitating food production - not advantages for the consumer.

Did you know? Food Intolerances and Leaky Gut*

Our gut lining is protected by thousands of "villi" that look like little nodules and act as a protective barrier between the gut and the circulatory system. Digested food particles are able to pass through the gut into the blood stream in a body friendly form. In certain circumstances, the gut wall can become leaky. A leaky gut allows the passage of undigested foods - and other toxins - into the circulatory system, provoking an immune response. This can explain some food intolerances.

Causes of Leaky Gut:

- High intake of wheat and dairy products - the proteins in them are especially hard to digest
- High alcohol intake
- Overgrowth of bad bacteria in the gut
- High intake of paracetamol.

The increase in the number of people suffering from food intolerances is thought to be linked to the lack of balance in our modern diet, with its overemphasis on sugar, wheat and dairy products. Another cause of leaky gut may be the early weaning of wheat and dairy into a baby's diet. It takes up to a year for a baby's gut to form fully - babies automatically have a leaky gut up until this happens. Some nutritionists argue that wheat and dairy products may be extremely difficult for babies to digest before this time and introducing wheat and dairy products too early may provoke an allergic reaction causing food intolerances further down the line.

* Note: Leaky gut is only one possible cause of food intolerances.

If you are concerned that you may have a food intolerance, please contact Yorktest laboratories on 0800 074 6185 or visit their website www.yorktest.com

Part IV – Cooking Methods and Good Nutrition

"Cookery is both an art form and a pleasure. If it is done well, the look and flavour of many foods is enhanced. However, as soon as the food is subjected to heat, its nutrient level can diminish... We need to establish a balance between flavour and nutrient value."
- Ian Marber & Vicki Edgson, The Food Doctor

Food is delicate. Its nutritional value is affected by the many different processes it goes through before it lands up on your plate! Some methods of cooking are better than others for preserving the nutrient content and water levels in food. Heat is the main culprit, and the more you do to food with heat, the more likely it will be that the nutritional value is reduced through destroying many valuable nutrients and enzymes contained within it.

Tip: Boiling Vegetables

The less water you use the better, and the larger the surface area of the vegetables the better. Finally, the shorter the time you boil the vegetables the better. By doing this, less nutrients are leached into the water and more are contained in the vegetables.

Cooking Method	Effect on Nutritional Value of Food
Raw	This is a fantastic way of eating food as nothing has been done to alter the goodness it contains. This obviously only applies to some food, for example fruit and vegetables!
Steaming	An excellent method of preserving the nutrient content of food.
Boiling	Water soluble nutrients may leach into the water. See "Boiling Vegetables" to learn how to minimise losses. Using the cooking water for soups and stews is a good way of retaining the nutrients transferred to the water.
Stewing and Casseroling	An excellent way of preserving nutrients - because most are captured in the sauce. Also, cooking at lower temperatures (but for longer periods of time) helps maintain the nutrient content.
Deep Frying	Requires high temperature cooking causing oxidation of fats and creating trans fats. Burnt food is also a source of carcinogens, whatever the cooking method.
Stir Frying	A preferable way to fry. Shorter cooking time preserves nutrients.
Microwaving	Only small nutrient losses, but there are concerns about how the structural integrity of food might be compromised leading to the production of harmful free-radicals.

Part V
The **COOK** Way

Edward's Guiding Principles when he set up **COOK**:

- We will use skilled chefs to cook the food, not machines.

- We will only cook in small batch sizes to retain the homemade taste and character of the meals.

- We will only use the best natural ingredients, and will never cook with any artificial ingredients.

- We will use nature's way of "preserving" - freezing

COOK is "Slow Food" disguised as "Fast Food"

You may have heard about the "slow food" movement that started in Italy. The movement's key premise is that good food needs time.

All too often, mass manufacturing methods squeeze out the inherent goodness - and pleasure - found in food.

We regularly talk about how **COOK** food is like cooking at home - because of the quality of the ingredients we use; and because we cook in kitchens, not factories. The reason we bang on about this so much is that it DOES make a difference to the quality of our food - and the associated health benefits. We get very touchy when we are referred to as a "ready meal". Because, although we provide meals that are "ready to eat", we have little else in common with most other ready meals!

We get very touchy when we are referred to as a "ready meal". Because, although we do provide meals that are "ready to eat", we have little else in common with most other "ready meals".

There are many health benefits of the **COOK** Way. But to be clear, we are not saying that we are a "health food" in the sprouting bean sense of the word! What we do provide is good, honest, unadulterated, delicious food that can form part of a balanced diet.

There are a number of things we do, which have a significant positive nutritional effect on our food:

- The quality of our ingredients is high
- We cook on a small scale
- What we don't put into the food is as important as what we do
- Freezing is nature's way of preserving and keeping food nutritionally rich.

At **COOK** we provide good, honest, unadulterated food that can form part of a balanced diet.

Many of
our vegetables are
cooked and frozen within
three days of being
harvested. This maximises
the optimum nutrient
levels of freshly
harvested produce.

The **COOK** Range

The **COOK** menu provides you with an excellent range of meals to help you ensure you are getting a healthy, varied diet.

A large proportion of our meals are "casserole" dishes. Casseroles and stews are extremely healthy because all nutrients are sealed into the sauce.
Try: Moroccan Lamb Tagine or Coq au Vin

We have a good selection of chicken dishes - an excellent "lean" source of protein. Especially as we remove the skin and trim off any fat before cooking.
Try: Pesto Chicken with Roasted Mediterranean Vegetables or Green Thai Chicken.

Although high intake is strongly associated with heart disease and obesity, lean red meat is an excellent source of protein, B vitamins and iron.
Try: Beef Bourguignonne or Spicy Italian Style Meatballs

Fish - such as cod and haddock - provides an extremely low fat source of protein. Oily fish such as salmon and trout are an excellent source of Omega 3 essential fatty acids.
Try: Hearty Fisherman's Pie or Moroccan Spiced Fish Tagine

Pulses & Legumes such as lentils and beans are "super healthy" - an excellent source of minerals, B vitamins and fibre.
Try: Red Lentil and Mixed Bean Casserole or Vegetable and Bean Chilli

Vegetable dishes that can be used both as main courses and side dishes. Our excellent range helps you meet your fruit and vegetable intake targets - remember eating enough vegetables (aim for 4 portions a day) is essential for optimum health.
Try: Vegetable Tagine or Wild Mushroom Stroganoff.

COOK uses olive oil in many of its dishes providing healthy monounsaturated fat.

COOK's casseroles and stews are healthy because they seal all the nutrients into the sauce.

We are pretty obsessive about the quality of our ingredients. Apart from making great tasting food, good quality ingredients have huge benefits on the nutritional value of our food. Here's why...

Vegetables

Trevor, our greengrocer, goes to New Covent Garden Market at 3am every day to buy our ingredients. He only buys the freshest and best quality vegetables that he can lay his hands on. He doesn't mind if the carrot isn't a beautiful shape, but he does mind that it is in perfect condition.

Trevor our greengrocer with our butcher, fishmonger and Head Chef

Wherever possible, Trevor buys UK vegetables, which will commonly have been picked the previous day. He delivers them to COOK's Kitchens at 9am every morning. We use them in our cooking either immediately or the following day. Many of our vegetables are cooked and frozen within three days of being harvested.

Nutritional Benefit: The fresher the vegetable, the higher its nutritional content. See 'The Lifespan of a Vegetable', page 33.

COOK's vegetables are selected for quality and freshness... not symmetry!

Meat

Our chefs are very particular about the quality of the meat they cook with. For example, they insist on Irish beef because they are unanimous that it cooks and tastes better than cheaper "New World" sources. Here's a summary of the nutritional benefits of our meat preparation:

Hand dicing -

It is common in mass manufacturing processes to "machine dice" meat. However, we dice our meat by hand - as this is the only way of getting all the excess fat off.

Nutritional benefit: Fat removed meat has as much as 30% lower saturated fat content. Toxins or antibiotic residues tend to reside in fatty tissue - removing fat by hand removes such toxins.

All our fresh ingredients are "checked in" by Ken, who is a trained chef with over 30 years experience. We don't just have a "goods in man" accepting deliveries. Ken assesses whether the quality of the produce is good enough - and as one of our valued chefs, he has very high standards.

Mincing -

We refuse to use "bought in" mince... we buy the prime cuts, trim them by hand and mince them ourselves. This ensures top quality lean mince and we know exactly what's gone into it!

Nutritional Benefit: High quality mince with lower saturated fat levels.

Chicken -

We source chicken from the EU. Many "ready meals" use chickens reared in the Far East and then "tumbled" - where the meat is processed through machines to fill it with water. Our chicken is reared without growth hormones, and with minimal antibiotics, minimising the "anti-nutrient" content. The chickens we use live in an "open paddock" under cover, but are not classed as free range.

Nutritional Benefit: High quality meat which is low in toxins or anti-nutrients.

Where our Meat and Fish comes from:

Wherever possible, we source from small, local suppliers. Sometimes, due to the quantities we require, we cannot source as locally as we would like. Lamb being the prime (pardon the pun!) example. If you know a Welsh farmer that can supply the quantity and quality of lamb we require, we'd love to hear from you!

Beef	Ireland
Lamb	New Zealand
Chicken	Holland
Duck	France
Pork	England
Cod	Iceland (from Sustainable Sources)
Salmon	Scotland

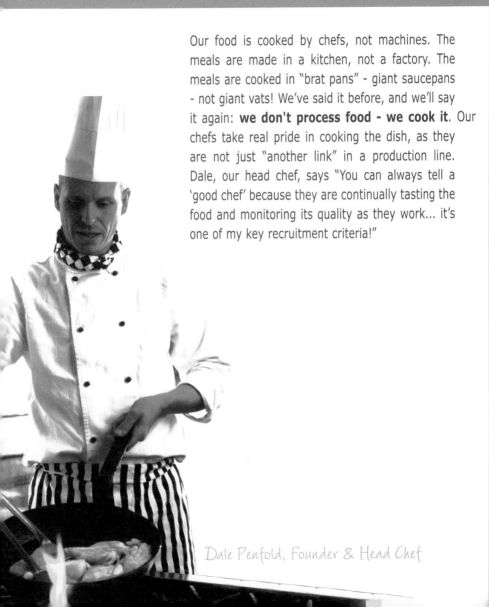

Our food is cooked by chefs, not machines. The meals are made in a kitchen, not a factory. The meals are cooked in "brat pans" - giant saucepans - not giant vats! We've said it before, and we'll say it again: **we don't process food - we cook it**. Our chefs take real pride in cooking the dish, as they are not just "another link" in a production line. Dale, our head chef, says "You can always tell a 'good chef' because they are continually tasting the food and monitoring its quality as they work... it's one of my key recruitment criteria!"

Dale Penfold, Founder & Head Chef

COOK Recipe – Lamb Moussaka

Perhaps the best way to explain how we do things is to talk you through making a typical dish, the **COOK** way:

Ingredients:

Lamb, milk, potatoes, aubergine, tomatoes, mature cheddar cheese, onions, tomato purée, regato cheese, flour, olive oil, butter, lamb bouillon, parsley, Worcestershire sauce, garlic, lemon juice, English mustard, oregano.

We trim off any excess fat from the meat by hand - just as you would at home. This can reduce the saturated fat content by 30%

1 Legs of lamb, rather than minced lamb, arrive at our kitchens. We like to mince the lamb ourselves, which allows us to remove any excess fat and therefore keep the meat as lean as possible. This means that there is a double check on the quality of our meat: The butcher will have chopped off any obvious fat before delivering the legs to us, but we remove any remaining fat by hand. This helps us to keep the saturated fat content to a minimum.

2 The vegetables are prepared using hand methods or small scale processing equipment (like a Magi mix), allowing us to continually measure the quality of these ingredients. In other words, if there's a mushroom that's looking a bit weary, the chef chucks it out. This means that we have two checks that are monitored by people (not machines!) to ensure that the vegetables are in superb condition.

We have two checks that are monitored by people (not machines!) that make sure that the vegetables are in superb condition. First, Trevor selects our vegetables at market daily. Our chef selects them again, when cooking.

The onions are sweated in oil and then the mince is added and cooked until tender. This ensures that maximum flavour is achieved and the nutrient content is sealed into the food. The fat is strained off: removing some of the saturated fat level. The other ingredients are added and gently simmered for half an hour. It would be quicker and more "efficient" to flash fry the dish, but more fat would then be added into the dish and we would lose all the valuable nutrients - not to mention the delicious flavour.

COOK relies on chefs and natural ingredients - not synthetic flavour enhancers - to give our meals their flavour and consistency.

The dish then goes through a sampling panel - to ensure we've achieved the right flavour and consistency. This is carried out by trained chefs and of course any adjustments that need to be made take place at this stage - a bit of extra pepper or oregano might be added here.

The fresh potatoes are sliced and steamed and laid one by one on the top of the dish which is brushed with a little butter - so that it browns nicely at home.

The dish is then ready to eat - but not before it's frozen... see more later!

What we don't put into our food

- No Artificial Preservatives*
- No Artificial Additives*
- No Artificial Flavour Enhancers*
- No Artificial Emulsifiers*
- No Artificial Stabilisers*
- No Artificial Colourings*
- No Modified Maize Starch*
- No Genetically Modified Ingredients ("GMOs")

Additives and artificial ingredients compromise immunity, load up toxins in the body and can contribute to a number of health-related ills.

COOK food is much healthier and better for you, because we do not "add in" these artificial ingredients ourselves.

Health benefits of keeping "The Artificials Out"

All of these additives tend to be used by food manufacturers to extend shelf life, or make production easier. They have little or no nutritional value and can usually be classed as anti-nutrients. They compromise immunity, load up toxins in the body and can contribute to a number of health related ills. Our food is much healthier and better for you, because we do not "add in" these artificial ingredients ourselves. As we have said before, we may make meals that are ready to eat, but we have little else in common with most other "ready meals".

What are Artificial Additives and Preservatives?
Synthetic chemicals added to food to extend shelf life, facilitate food preparation and make food more appealing - by enhancing colour, flavour and texture.

What are Artificial Flavour Enhancers?
Synthetic chemicals that trick the taste buds into thinking a food has more flavour than it does. The best known flavour enhancer is MSG (monosodium glutamate) commonly used in Chinese cuisine.

What are Artificial Emulsifiers and Stabilisers?
Synthetic chemicals added to food to prevent the separation of water and oil and generally maintain the food in the "desired form".

What are Artificial Colours?
Pretty self-evidently, artificial colours are added to food to enhance or produce a desired colour.

What is Modified Maize Starch?
A synthetic "thickener" often used to thicken foods in mass manufacturing food production. We use cornflour or a roux (equal amounts of butter and flour) instead.

* You may have noticed that we do have some artificial emulsifiers, additives, preservatives etc on our labels. This is because these ingredients are present in some of the products we use (tomato puree etc). However, we use the same "dry products" you probably have at home in the cupboard. We declare it as an ingredient but it is only "carried over" from other products in exactly the same way that it would be present if you used these ingredients when cooking for your family.

We are on a constant mission to minimise the additives and preservatives that are carried over from our ingredients into our meals, and wherever possible, we do so. However, sometimes it is simply not possible to make a dish that does not use an ingredient which will carry over some additives and preservatives.

Once we have finished cooking a meal, we immediately chill it, then "blast freeze" it at -25°C. Freezing is nature's way of preserving and has health benefits because it doesn't rely on anything being "added" to preserve the food (such as artificial preservatives or artificial stabilisers). Many preservation methods significantly alter the nutrient content of food - just like certain cooking processes can tamper with the nutrient content of food - but freezing has little effect on it.

"Freezing can actually help preserve levels of certain nutrients in the food, as the nutrient concentrations are placed in 'suspended animation' whilst the produce remains frozen"
- British Nutrition Foundation

This is particularly true when food is blast frozen - an extremely high proportion of the nutrient value of the food is sealed in. Blast freezing is key, because on a molecular level, if a food is frozen rapidly only "small ice crystals" are formed. However, if food is frozen slowly, larger ice crystals have the opportunity to form. When the meal is reheated, smaller ice crystals have little effect on the taste and quality of the food and its nutrients, large crystals are much more damaging.

"Ever since the advent of the home freezer, sensible cooks have rustled up wholesome casseroles in hefty quantities: some to eat now, some to be frozen for another day. And while home freezers take an average of 12 hours to completely freeze food, commercial blast freezing does the job so quickly that nutrients and flavours are sealed inside before they have a chance to deteriorate."

- The Food Detective, The Times 2005

Nutritional Content of Our Food

We have full print-outs of the nutritional contents of our food available in our shops. For a quick reference, here are some of the "top scorers" in terms of fat, saturated fat, salt and calories. We hope you find these rankings helpful when making decisions about what to eat, based on your individual nutritional needs.

By the way: These Top 20 rankings exclude our entertaining dishes, vegetable side dishes and our puddings - they are designed to help you choose healthy main courses for everyday use.

All values in the league tables are correct at the time of printing. Please note that because we are continually improving our recipes, there may be slight variations in nutritional values over time. If in doubt, please refer to the label.

Did you know?
Guideline Daily Amounts

Guideline Daily Amounts are used to help people understand the level of nutrients they are eating - some food producers state nutritional values on labels as a percentage of these GDAs. The thing to remember is that GDAs are guidelines that have been drawn up for average adults. Individual requirements will vary depending on age, weight and level of activity.

Guideline Daily Amounts

Each Day	Women	Men
Calories	2000KCal	2500KCal
Fat	70g	95g
Saturated Fat	20g	30g

The maximum daily intake of salt for an average adult is 6g, or 2.4g of sodium.

Top 20 Lowest Calorie Meals

Dish	Kcal per Portion
1. Fish and Roasted Vegetable Kebabs	189
2. Chicken & Roasted Vegetable Kebabs	228
3. Vegetable Tagine	246
4. Chilli con Carne	255
5. Red Thai Chicken	269
6. Red Lentil and Mixed Bean Casserole	273
7. Lamb Bordeaux	276
8. Moroccan Spiced Fish Tagine	278
9. Beef Bourguignonne	285
10. Chicken Jalfrezi	288
11. Green Thai Chicken	298
12. Lime and Coriander Stuffed Trout	305
13. Beef Goulash	314
14. Nut Loaf	328
15. Tarragon and Orange Chicken	338
16. Moroccan Lamb Tagine	360
17. Wild Mushroom Stroganoff	363
18. Spicy Italian-style Meatballs	364
19. Honey Roast Duck in Plum Sauce	368
20. Pesto Chicken	370

The Guideline Daily Amount
is
2000Kcal for women
and
2500Kcal for men

Top 20 Lowest Fat Meals

Dish	g Fat per 100g
1. Red Thai Chicken	2.9
2. Chilli con Carne	3.4
3. Moroccan Lamb Tagine	3.5
4. Chicken Jalfrezi	3.5
5. Green Thai Chicken	3.8
6. Beef Bourguignonne	3.9
7. Beef Goulash	4.0
8. Red Lentil and Mixed Bean Casserole	4.0
9. Vegetable Tagine	4.1
10. Moroccan Spiced Fish Tagine	4.4
11. Chicken and Tomato Pasta Bake	4.5
12. Shepherd's Pie	4.8
13. Honey Roast Duck in Plum Sauce	4.9
14. Lamb Bordeaux	5.0
15. Spicy Italian-style Meatballs	5.1
16. Pesto Chicken	5.2
17. Lasagne Verde	5.3
18. Steak and Red Wine Pie (small)	5.3
19. Tarragon and Orange Chicken	5.3
20. Huntsman's Chicken	5.5

The Food Standards Agency
recommends that, per 100g:

0-3g is a little amount or "low fat"
3-20g is a moderate amount
20g and over is a lot of fat

Top 20 Lowest Saturated Fat Meals

Dish	g Saturated Fat per 100g
Chicken Jalfrezi	0.5
Vegetable Tagine	0.5
Red Lentil and Mixed Bean Casserole	0.6
Steak and Red Wine Pie (small)	0.8
Lamb Bordeaux	0.8
Beef Bourguignonne	0.9
Moroccan Spiced Fish Tagine	1.0
Pesto Chicken	1.0
Red Thai Chicken	1.1
Fish and Roasted Vegetable Kebabs	1.1
Spaghetti Bolognaise	1.2
Moroccan Lamb Tagine	1.2
Chicken & Roasted Vegetable Kebabs	1.2
Honey Roast Duck in Plum Sauce	1.4
Chilli con Carne	1.5
Beef Goulash	1.6
Green Thai Chicken	1.8
Spicy Italian-style Meatballs	1.9
Lime and Coriander Stuffed Trout	1.9
Vegetable Moussaka	2.1

The Food Standards Agency recommends that, per 100g:

0-1g is a little amount of saturated fat
1-5g is a moderate amount of saturated fat
5g or more is a lot of saturated fat

Top 20 Lowest Salt Meals

Dish	g Salt per 100g
Fish and Roasted Vegetable Kebabs	0.1
Beef Goulash	0.2
Salmon and Asparagus Bake	0.3
Wild Mushroom Stroganoff	0.3
Vegetable Korma	0.3
Vegetable Tagine	0.4
Chicken & Roasted Vegetable Kebabs	0.4
Braised Lamb Shanks	0.4
Red Lentil and Mixed Bean Casserole	0.4
Hearty Fisherman's Pie	0.4
Steak and Red Wine Pie (small)	0.5
Honey Roast Duck in Plum Sauce	0.5
Tarragon and Orange Chicken	0.5
Red Thai Chicken	0.5
Braised Beef Diane	0.5
Spicy Italian-style Meatballs	0.5
Green Thai Chicken	0.5
Pesto Chicken	0.5
Cottage Pie	0.5
Chicken Alexander	0.5

The Food Standards Agency recommends that, per 100g:

0-0.25g is a little amount of salt
0.25g-1.25g is a moderate amount
1.25g or more is high in salt

Know Your Labels

Example: Beef Bourguignonne

Ingredients are listed in order of weight – greatest first.

We have relaunched our labels to give you more nutritional information! Each label now shows: Calories, Protein, Carbohydrate, Carbohydrate of which sugars, Fat, Saturated Fat, Fibre and Salt as Sodium contents for each dish.

Ingredients:

SILVERSIDE OF BEEF (52%) : WATER: SMOKED BACON (12%): MUSHROOMS ((10%): BUTTON ONIONS (9%): TOMATO JUICE (Tomatoes, Salt, Citric Acid): ONION PUREE (Tomatoes, Salt): VEGETABLE OIL: PLAIN WHEAT FLOUR: BEEF STOCK (Contains: Beef (38%)): PORT: GARLIC: MUSHROOM STOCK (Contains: Mushrooms (min 30%)): GRAVY BROWNING (Contains: Water, Caramel): THYME, DEMERARA SUGAR: RED WINE VINEGAR: PEPPER: BAY LEAVES

All appliances vary, the following are guidelines only. For best results always cook from frozen.

Oven

1. Pre-heat oven to 180°C / fan-assisted oven 160°C / 350°F / gas mark 4.
2. Remove cardboard sleeve & pierce film lid several times.
3. Place on a baking tray & cook in the centre of the oven for 40-45 minutes.
4. Ensure the food is piping hot before serving.

- -

Microwave

Remove sleeve & pierce film lid several times. Place on a microwaveable plate & cook on full power, following the guidelines below:
650W (CATEGORY B)
Cook for 4 minutes, partially peel back film & stir, replace film, cook for 3 minutes, stir, cook for 1 minute.
850W (CATEGORY E)
Cook for 3 minutes, partially peel back film lid & stir, replace film, cook for 2 minutes, stir, cook for 1 minute.

Caution: Steam may be released when removing film lid.

NUTRITION INFORMATION

Typical Values	Per 100g	Per Portion 290g
Energy Kj	398.0	1194.0
Energy Kcal	95.0	285.0
Protein g	10.0	30.0
Carbohydrate g	3.7	11.1
of which sugars g	1.3	3.9
Fat g	3.9	11.7
of which saturates g	0.9	2.7
Fibre g	0.4	1.2
Sodium g	0.2	0.6

Per portion 285.0 calories 11.7g fat 1.6g salt

Allergen Information
Product contains: gluten & wheat
This product has been made in a kitchen which uses nut ingredients.

Should this product defrost, keep refrigerated & eat within 2 days. Follow the oven guidelines & cook for 20-25 minutes.

5 060028 700158

As always, we also show you how to cook the meal – both in your oven and also in a microwave, if possible.

Any allergen information is clearly stated.

Each label also gives a summary of the Fat, Salt and Calorie content per portion.

Summing Up...

Ever since Dale and I first started **COOK** back in 1996, we have always believed that food should be prepared using fresh ingredients and proper cooking techniques. It was an instinctive belief - mainly motivated by taste! The traditional nutritional value (protein/carbohydrate/fat/salt/sugar) of our food is mixed in the sense that many dishes are extremely healthy, some are moderately good for you and a few don't rate quite so highly (but are fine to be eaten in a balanced way). In fact, as we've been saying for years, eating our food is much like cooking for yourself at home.

Good nutrition is about much more than just the statistics on the label - and our instincts were right that food made by people (not machines), cooked in small batches using natural ingredients with no artificial flavours or preservatives is, on so many levels, better for our wellbeing than all of the alternatives, other than cooking, from scratch, for yourself.

What we have tried to do in this guide is to give you a general overview on nutrition, and point you in the direction of good sources of additional information if you are particularly interested in a topic. Ultimately, we hope that as a result of reading this guide you will be better able to make informed decisions about your diet. And obviously, we hope that you will continue to enjoy our delicious and nutritious food as part of a balanced diet!

Edward

Edward Perry - Founder

About the Author

In the autumn of 2004, when **COOK** was looking for someone to write a nutrition guide, my new wife, Jenny, very unwisely started to show an interest in this project. In traditional **COOK** style, she was "requisitioned" to write the guide.

Jen has always had an interest in nutrition, well-being and health, and was already pretty knowledgeable about certain areas of the topic. She has really enjoyed researching this area in full. Jenny would like to thank Lesley McLauchlan, an excellent Clinical Nutritionist, for her invaluable advice on the guide.

Brown rice - still, mercifully, with lots of our food - is now a regular feature on our evening menu at home, and it's delicious!

James Perry (MD)

64

Benefits of **COOK** Food

- Excellent range offering you healthy alternatives for a varied and balanced diet.

- Fresh vegetables selected daily at market.

- High quality, lean cuts of meat delivered daily and prepared just as you would at home.

- Chefs not machines mean food is cooked, not processed.

- Freezing - Nature's way of preserving.

- No Artificial Additives, Preservatives, Emulsifiers, Colourings added in by our chefs.

Books

"The Food Doctor" - Ian Marber & Vicki Edgson
"The New Optimum Nutrition Bible" - Patrick Holford
"You Are What You Eat" - Dr Gillian McKeith
"The G.I. Guide" - Rick Gallop & Hamish Renton
"Fats that Heal, Fats That Kill" - Udo Erasmus
"Not On The Label" - Felicity Lawrence
"Shopped" - Joanna Blythman
"The Atlas of Food" - Erik Millstone & Tim Lang

Websites

www.eatwell.gov.uk .....Sponsored by the Food Standards Agency. An excellent source of information on all issues relating to nutrition.
www.fsa.gov.uk ....Food Standards Agency website
www.salt.gov.uk ........F.S.A. site dedicated to salt
www.nutrition.org.uk ....British Nutrition Foundation website
www.coeliac.co.uk ....Support site for those suffering from coeliac's disease
www.diabetes.org.uk .....Support site for those suffering from diabetes
www.edauk.com ....Eating Disorders Association website
www.wholefoods.com ....Contains excellent nutrition reference library
www.healthcastle.com ...Excellent general source for nutrition information
www.slowfood.com ......Site of the international "Slow Food" movement
www.foodcomm.org.uk ...Site of The Food Commission, an N.G.O. campaigning for safer and healthier food in the U.K.
www.patrickholford.com ..Site of the nutrition expert, Patrick Holford.

*"Be careful about reading health books.
You may die of a misprint".*

- Mark Twain (1835-1910)

ISBN 0-9551063-0-3

www.cookfood.net/nutrition

COOK Trading Limited, 84 High Street, Tonbridge, Kent TN9 1AP

Tel: 0870 048 9305   Email: nutrition@cookfood.net

9 780955 106309